TRACKS

By the same author

(2020) *Pistes de rêve*. Editions du Petit Véhicule.
(2020) *Kaosmos*. MPU.
(2019) *After Cage*. Girls on Key.
(2019) *Kosmogonies*. Encres Vives.
(2018) *Hors limites*. L'Harmattan.
(2018) with Béatrice Machet. *Crypto*. Flying Islands Press.
(2018) with Julian Novitz, eds. *Creative Writing with Critical Theory: Inhabitation*. Gylphi.
(2017) *Hush: A Fugue*. UWA Publishing.
(2015) *Towards a Poetics of Creative Writing*. Multilingual Matters.
(2015) with Russell Grigg and Craig Smith, eds. *Female Sexuality: The Early Psychoanalytic Controversies*. Karnac.
(2014) *Stretchmarks of Sun*. Re.Press.
(2012) *The Creativity Market: Creative Writing in the 21st Century*. Multilingual Matters.
(2009) *Out of Bounds*. Re.Press.
(2006) *Couchgrass*. Papyrus Publishing.
(2004) *Noisy Blood: Stories*. Papyrus Publishing.
(2002) *Good Grief*. Papyrus Publishing.
(2000) *The Book of Elsa*. Papyrus Publishing.
(2000) *Magic and Other Stories*. Woorilla.
(1999) with Russell Grigg and Craig Smith *Female Sexuality: The Early Psychoanalytic Controversies*. Rebus Press.
(1999) *The Gaze of Silence*. Sidewalk Collective.
(1999) *Mythfits: Four Uneasy Pieces*. PenFolk Publishing.

TRACKS

autofictional fragments of a journey without maps

(1985-2015)

DOMINIQUE HECQ

RECENT
WORK
PRESS

Tracks
Recent Work Press
Canberra, Australia

Copyright © Dominique Hecq, 2020

ISBN: 9780648936732 (paperback)

 A catalogue record for this book is available from the National Library of Australia

All rights reserved. This book is copyright. Except for private study, research, criticism or reviews as permitted under the Copyright Act, no part of this book may be reproduced, stored in a retrieval system, or transmitted in any form by any means without prior written permission. Enquiries should be addressed to the publisher.

Cover image: 'Great Southern Land' by Alexander Gerst, reproduced under Creative Commons Attribution-ShareAlike 2.0 Generic
Cover design: Recent Work Press
Set by Recent Work Press

recentworkpress.com

SS

It was the valley itself that drew Voss. Its mineral splendours were increased in that light. As bronze retreated, veins of silver loomed in the gullies, knobs of amethyst and sapphire glowed on the hills

Patrick White

Contents

fo‿(e)₁woɹd	1
making tracks	5
arrivals	13
leavings	27
OutsIde the beaten track	39
traversals	65
faultlines	89
traces...	105

This is a work of fiction inspired by a real journey. Names, characters, places and incidents are either the product of the author's imagination or are used fictitiously. Any resemblance to actual events, locales or persons is coincidental and beyond the intent of author and publisher.

for(e)word

This book begins in Brussels, April 1974: through with an essay on Voltaire's *Candide,* and snug at my grandparents' house, I watch a film called *A Town like Alice*. Not at all what I expected, though it is some kind of wonderland—leathery earth flattened in my dreams; a deep blue sky that doesn't curve. I want to go to Alice.

This book begins in London, July 1982. I've just seen a documentary about the Australian Aborigines: how they were segregated in reserves, how their children were taken from their mothers, how their dreamtime stories disappeared on the horizon line in the name of civilisation and God. I seek out Australians. Cam tells me I am mistaken: there are no reserves, no missions, no ... not in Australia. I feel affronted. Seek out books about Australian history. Read works by Australian writers: Patrick White bowls me over.

From *Voss*, I move on to *A Fringe of Leaves*, reading fiction against facts, history against mythology. At Australia House, I discover Randolph Stow in whose haunted landscapes figure missions and missionaries and Aborigines. *To the Islands* moves me beyond words and I am fascinated by the language, especially towards the end of the novel, when the protagonist, Heriot, a missionary, sings in the midst of his delirium a wild corroboree about himself, as though ghosting himself on his way to the islands of the dead. I am entranced. Then I chance upon Robert Drewe's *The Savage Crows*. I hatch a plan: I will write on the representation of Aborigines in Australian fiction.

In 1985 I fly over to Australia, to take up a scholarship and write a PhD on Australian literature with little baggage but my faux-Romantic prejudices.

Tracks fictionalises the journey in a sequence of poems that span thirty years of autobiographical fragments exploring what it means to belong.

making tracks

                              It begins with an omen

A clap of thunder

Fat drops of rain

We hurry into the British Museum
walk through each room until she
catches us, Truganini

        Her eyes bore through the glass, accusing

People gather around us

We run out into ropes of rain

                        Through the gates

Our hands part

We enter an antiquarian bookshop

A smell of dust, papyri and methylated spirits

You quote Havelock
            splayed out on a lectern:

the habit of using written symbols to represent [...] speech is just a useful trick which has existed over too short a span of time to have been built into our genes, whether or not this may happen half a million years hence. In short, reading man, as opposed to speaking man, is not biologically determined

It comes from afar and carries through us
some unnatural history of selection
                (I know better than to ask about speaking
                reading or writing woman)

Our feet walk us to Highgate

At the theatrette

We chance upon *We of the Never Never*

Watch, squirming in silence

Decide to stay for the documentary

We head to the bar
    argue
        about the (non)existence of Aboriginal reserves

Oh, how I insult the Church Fathers, your country, your family
Oh, how you riposte with statistics of the Congo

I go out for a smoke

Wind blows from the south

At Gatwick we promise to keep in touch

I hurry back to Highgate
a copy of *Flaws in the Glass* under my arm
                              in my hand a map of Australia

I'm in love

I read *Voss, A Fringe of Leaves, Arcady in Australia, Triumph of the Nomads, To the Islands, Tourmaline, The Savage Crows*

Cry for the Dead

We do not write, or call

I see *The Chant of Jimmie Blacksmith, Picnic at Hanging Rock Man of Flowers*

I read *The Fortunes of Richard Mahony, My Brilliant Career*

Such is Life

For Love Alone

I book a one-way ticket to Melbourne

.

(...)

I bid goodbye to the *whited sepulchre*
of my native land

Drink a Stella Artois
off *Rue de la Loi*

Breath condensing on the glass
I cheer the absent

                (if I think of words like
                choice of nightmares, yes
                I repress them right away)

                        At the *Musée des Beaux Arts*

I purchase a notebook
pocket the French language

20 February 1985

(advice to self)

Stick to the letter A
    but mind it's hybridised

Aircraft boarding is a last minute affair
    (Australia is a long way)

Appraise fellow passengers
Attachez vos ceintures / Fasten seatbelts
Listen to *Air*

Abu Dhabi is for attending to natural needs only
    (forty minutes to find your gate)

At Tullamarine's A terminal, clap
Amble through customs
Look for Andrew

If late, remember it's the Aussie way
    and listen to the local lingo while you wait

Don't worry about the ubiquitous letter F

arrivals

Andrew picks me up in his *yoot*
                (he's late)
I can't bring myself to call him Andy
                (he is a Professor)

My ears strain to attune to new sounds

Andrew keeps saying *eggs jelly*
talks about an eminent *gess vonner* from *Sinney Yooney*

I look through the window

We shoot through a makeshift landscape—wayward
fields of concrete, rusty skies over rows of identical boxes tearing
through glare past loud billboards and neon signs

Then, *Mirabile Dictu*, Andy does a *uey* and as we swing around
I figure what *dent shoe worry* means
terror souse and *scona rayn*
      (I try not to worry)

Higgledy-piggledy architecture

Brick-veneer houses vie with weatherboard bungalows, wrought-iron verandas, carports, granny flats, pubs, car-yards and graveyards, milk-bars, bottle-shops, drive-ins. Jasmine and bougainvilleas clambering fences. Hills Hoists sporting carnivals of colours. Ravens and magpies. A prison. Community halls, bowling lawns, construction sites. Motels. MacDonalds.

Suburban gothic

Gumtrees. The bush, at last! Wait. A car park like a runway

The University: *no roos ere, only blowies 'n chtewdence*

In the Arts Buliding we meet *chair-free* who smells of beer, Sue who *kenardly bleevit* and *chiffon* who tells me to *tiger teasy*
                                            (I try to take it easy)

Left behind, bleak days
a snow-smothered land

Here spindle trees rise
pale as dancers in a tumble
of colours I can't name

Here wind and light lift
the sky to breaking point

Here spindle trees rise
pale as dancers in a Sidney Long

Here wind and light scour
the backbone of the earth

Here all fake certainties
vanish with language

Light pours down
the unrelenting sky

To earth ridged
with Van Gogh brush strokes

I track words
for hues and shades in books

Envy the skill of artist-explorers
who forged new ways of seeing

The cries of crows fall
on a Drysdale landscape

Blues on rusty ochres
pulse with dust

This place blinds my eyes
stills my tongue

Word comes there is a party
on the other side of town

A posie by the sea
all done up with a deck
hecky whecky you'll love it

I say I'll walk and you
piss yourself laughing
        (I'll hear later)

This is Oz-tray-lia la Belge
it's a looooong way to anywhere mayte

Here people offer booze, not Chianti
Chenin Blanc, Rioja, Shiraz, Ale or Bitter

Here people ask who I *barrack* for
                    (...)

Here I learn DIMENSION means don't mention (it)

Here I learn the words *cobber darl dag ocker* and *cracking*
                    (which they do a lot)

Here, *whacko*, I meet an indigenous archaeologist

Here I blush and learn to hold my tongue
        (you don't *research* the Aborigines)

Didn't the painter Glover once tell
of white men disturbing the peace?

Ask no questions
Tell no lies
Open your mouth
And catch the flies

Here pronouns get mixed up

Moomba!

You expect a feast
song, music, dance, poetry

But instead find yourself out of step
in a procession of freaks in loud garments
a succession of stalls selling hot dogs, doughnuts, burgers
a parade not unlike the *mardis gras* of your childhood
but for the *demo* of drunken behaviour and commotion
of disworded voices

gloria sty uh? yeggowan? wezzme hembag?
dint note was ya san iler calf trim
tram term night sear

You walk back to campus
the sun, a monkey on your back

Your first taste
               of the *tyranny of distance*
   (*it's a looooong way to anywhere mayte*)

Your feet are sore, your face is afire, all of you dusty

Cracked explorer

wine chevver cole share?

Yes, a cold shower to drown all that (…)

You want to like it all

Barbies, booze, drop-bears, bunyips, ghetto blasters
Hey Hey It's Saturday, Yes Prime Minister, Neighbours
Crocodile Dundee, AC-DC, Nick Cave, Midnight Oil
The Galapagos Ducks, The Queensland Youth Orchestra

Melbourne's confused weather, its wind, mildew, moths, deserted night streets, drunks who trip you and laugh away

Brisbane's heat, blowies giant mozzies, bats brawling in trees

Byron's rollers, dumpers, stingers, rocks and blue bottles

You want to love the bush, its corellas, crows, magpies, finches willy-wag-tails, eucalypts and skeleton trees

You want to prove Marcus Clarke wrong
                (that *Weird Melancholy*)

You write about sunrises rainbowing the sky

You peel the colours of gum leaves apart
                                    grey, green, blue
light, heavy, weightless greys; gingeli and ginger greens
cutting, melting and steaming blues; slow, loose indigos

You ask why artists don't stick around—
London, Paris, Greece, New York
Wowsers make them cringe, mayte

You argue against *the Cultural Cringe*

You throw out your dresses, heels, makeup
    buy boots, moleskins and a Drizabone

You hack off your hair
    learn to light a fire
    boil the billy
    bake damper
    smoke Capstan rollies

You enter another time
    encounter Leichhardt, Mitchell, Hume and Giles
    converse with Harpur
    ride out with Paterson
    drink with Kendall

You hear sounds depthless as Sarah Island's silence

You see things like rivers rushing upstream and lambent lights

You shed cells and pounds and chunks of your life go missing

You are a hiatus where time and space are interchangeable

You learn the word *time-warp*

Andy says you can't both adopt and undercut tradition
Friends say you're overworked, isolated, in shock

Word comes there is a party...

You have ceased enjoying
the passion for ignorance

You are angry and don't know why
    (call this a moment of clarity)

You are their bamboozled pet friend
the exotic item in their collection
        (the accented one)

You are the nerd

The (consenting) convenient fuck

Yet to become the scapegoated clan outsider

You have to find some way—I call it mythological—to find some real spiritual link between us and the landscape, us and the cities, us and the lives we live here... it's not ready-made—it has to be imagined

Us?

How many colonisers
have spoken in the name of *us*
                versus *land*
how many tyrants
have spoken in the name of *us*
                versus *them*
           spirit versus *flesh*

Us?

~~To make *us* see the store of meaning in the idea and the way in which to *imagine* a nation is to engage not in a dialogue, but in a conversation with people, life, the world~~

(Editor, January 2017)

You lie

(or is it *lay*?)

        head resting on your arms
        in the empty space of sand

Around you the beach crowd in polka dot bikinis
green and gold togs and board shorts all in shades of blue
sit and chat and run and screech as they tumble in the heat

The sand beneath your towel moulds
itself to the shape of your body

The sun stings your skin

You are oblivious to the squabbling of seagulls
                              thumping of waves

You are oblivious to the voices calling you

You are becoming other

leavings

Sentences break
        on the pebbles of my Australian accent

Big flat vowels *floy away-y*
        loyke chooks with clipped wings

She'll be royt mayte, oy

She's been away too long

ses voyelles s'envolent
her vowels fly away
        comme des poules aux ailes coupées
like chooks with clipped wings

Je / elle tombe à plat ventre dans la gadoue
I / she falls flat in the muck

(the expat wishes)

To begin again where she got lost
To scamper in the scrub like an emu chick
To skinny dip in the creek
To bask in the sparse melodies of bellbirds
To pluck plums from the ground and figs from the tree
To tunnel through overgrown vines
To make the colours of the setting sun scream
To gather pine cones that ignite the night
To listen to the timpani of rain on the tin roof
To watch the sky split with lightning
To fry field mushrooms that bleed black ink
To get drunk on poetry and mulled wine
To hold her breath lighting a match
To wake up to the shriek of wattle birds
To mock the world like a kookaburra
To let her hair down and sink all clichés
To rise with the unknown flat on her hand

St Denis, St Jacques, St Christophe, St Martin, Ste Marguerite

Soulless, I

Walk through the city of churches
                its cockroach crowds
scurrying to offices, desks, forms, stamps

Walk through streets shiny with grime
                sleet and coal dust

                              There's coffee and waffles, hot chips
                                  smoke, piss and dog shit
                                        in the air

Walk through laneways off laneways through
            cobbles, puddles, potholes, shadows
                whoosh, whoosh, whoosh
                      whoooosh

My feet have grown with Australia's size

I inscribe

                                                      paths with their soles
                                              like a nun doing penance

                                                                re-inscribe

            stories of home grown sour
head tilted
                    towards the Southern Cross

                                                          I catch
                                                  a strip of blue
                                             slowly unclouding

catch
a strip of grey
charcoaling

Specks of dust rust
metal particles   float

towards the surface
of skin, eye-balling
you, modelling for Braille

The heart creases
in the chest, its iron
filings   filling silence

Rose corollas
papery in the fading
light, scrape

of air sounds you
like a gong in the desert
the sun at tipping point

Act so that there is use in a centre

Daily accumulation of words

I rediscover the dictionary
carry on the business of living
a cage in my heart

I use black and red ink back
and forth back and forth

Life's a performance of hyper
realism evading worlding selves

stuck in a broken metronome

Act so that there is no use in a centre

Art doesn't come into the prod
uction of poetry for people lacking
flexibility unctuosity plasticity tract
ability

poets think structures
penfection, undo
disorder disarray disturbance dismay, nothing
significant, let alone
fundamental, prime
eval—vale evil, evacuation, vellum anchor
ing signs sighs un
marking

the invention of lexicons
reinventions of selves, all that
entanglement of legacies

We are constructed now
bound in this symbolic imaginary real

The Napoleonic code's repetitive
toccata, period

I disappear
in a fog of *Maleboroughs*

You snore next door
claiming all the air

Clouds ride across the sky
sabres clipping the moon's face

The world dissolves
in crimson cinders

DO NOT DISTURB

the order of the universe

Denn wir sind nur die Schale und das Blatt

I'm back planting shoots
in a back garden
where every blade of grass
switches off the sun
its two faces in my sky
five languages I can't hold

Be my Taxi rank seatbelt duty
free cigarettes boarding pass landing card

I miss the crust
of summers baked bald
crackle of cicadas
churn of the surf
the body's effortless
holding of breath
in a listless garden

Be my Charles Austin from bud to full blown flower

Be my hyphen

                                I watch seasons change
                                        years go past

I grow thin and cold
sprout a growth
not quite a child
tend tough roses that catch
their second wind without me
knowing their names

My hair falls
like autumn leaves
and the idea of me

les feuilles mortes se ramassent à la pelle

                    Be the finger that pulls the trigger

                                Be my last breath

OutsIde the beaten track

You worm your way through the valley
breathe in the camphorous haze
follow tracks under canopies of light and leaves

All around, the vertical extent of the rock walls

The insistent play of sun and water in the falls

High up in the sky, a wedge-tailed eagle circles

Eyes half focused on some faraway plain
glowing with *mineral splendour*, words tumble
disperse and reassemble in your head:

This is a land of surfeit and lack
of harshness and clarity of image
of absence that opens out
or closes up the world
and sometimes the heart

You know you'll never belong

Three years...

                      If photos were the subject
you look pre-Raphaelite in your silk dress
                        (necessarily off-white)
        he, cosmopolitan—a touch of Aussie
        larrikinism about the mouth and eyes

Soon Irish Catholicism ruled

            your home, your life, your body
              (he says it's the Australian way)

they're not us they're them they're them
they are else what you don't know
what you don't know what they
think they got their own ways

Soon you will be with child (again)

Cocooned in fog, you are
cold. This could be

Brussels, Liège, London
except here you can

make a fire, consume
Fisherman's Friend

cough drops against
a touch of flu. On the radio

is the ABC drive
time show *Kaleidoscope*

which seems to believe
listeners have tempo

rary lobotomies
for one hour every
afternoon

With five depleted languages
letters to your name
such a lovely accent

tell me what you do
in an Australian country town

First of all, pawn your jewellery
ghetto blaster, violin, first editions

(done)

If hungry, whistle away
time, space and the grit in between

(teeth ground to the gum)

Try baby-sitting. Apply
at the school, pool, child-care centre

And for goodness' sake, stop crying for the moon

There's always barista, bar tender, cleaner, sandwich hand

(no experience, no references)

Ask around

(here womenfolk don't go to work)

Stop whingeing

(get on with it, dear
cook your husband breakfast
have a cup of tea
two sugars in mine)

Kiss your arse good-bye, jump
in the lake

(beg your pardon?)

Find yourself an interpreter

In the sharp angled, white edged space
of a country hospital, they pass the child
from hand to hand, each to each in silence

As though scared to death
to hold the shape
weight, breath of their unkithed kin

No-one asks what we named her

All gather in the TV room to watch *the granny*

Your French's gone to the dogs, Arthur says
Poor dogs, Martha cracks
a smile. Four years away and a dead
child in the bargain. Can't expect much
more.

Haven't they fed the dingoes yet?
Don't act the dingo on me
mate, he barks. No-one likes
a bloody fake ya-Kitty-yak.

To a brick, she loses her cherry
They tie the knot, pissant
around like ping-pong balls
until they're skint. Souvenir
the idea of home.

Folk call them chalkies, bull
artists, dole bludgers: they just seem
like they collect colloquialisms
more than things

These city slickers wouldn't know
their arses from their elbows
Martha tells this *herbulist*
I say I'll learn Greek

Here the waters are real waters
however much they won't hold
still to be told
exactly where they begin

The earth is the real earth
there is no other
so cold on the fingers
so close to the bone

And these trees are real trees
not pale dots on the map

And the land of men talks crap
and the land of women moves on

You have become a fiction

You live as people do in novels
except there is no passion, ecstasy, danger
                        (only dejection)

You aren't quite
                disembodied and voiceless
                a bush moth hankering after city lights

Fair dinkum

You make your own maps
                push your way through the city from park to park
        playground to playground, swing to swing

The child holds on tight

You sing magpie songs, frog songs, cricket songs, roo songs, kingfisher songs and echidna songs
                                        Write into the dark

This is a city that shelters itself from the sea

This is a city of public gardens and monuments
bike tracks and churches
cricket pitches and football grounds

This is a city where sport is a religion
                    and religion is a sport

A city where traditions and their rituals create
inhibitions and prohibitions that stick
                            like clichés

We rise in the acrid scent of gumtrees
above the lake
strewn with red flecked swans

Lifted away, the russet tracks of paddocks
ridged and stubbled
tilt toward the sea

On a rim of blue sparkling in the sun
we wheel across a creek receding
into drought
towards the shore

Raw sunlight grazes
rows of houses stacked stone
on stone above the sea

A cool breeze along streets
laid out year on year

The red stain of earth
on our hands

The bleeding heart of baby Jesus
presumably one day old

The garbled words of cricket
commentary cushioning silence

The surplus of virtual motherlands
absence of real songlines

The child watches cricket on the telly
    says he needs an outfit like that
        but not the black mask

How do you explain race to a kid?

How do you explain the divisive notion
    at the core of *us* versus *them*?

You open *Remembering Babylon*

    encounter Gemmy balanced

        on the top rail of a fence

Do not shoot, you read
    I am a B-b-british object!

~~Skinny Gemmy sat on a fence~~
~~Skinny Gemmy fell under a spell~~
~~And all the letters in the alphabet~~
~~And all the myths of the spell binder~~
~~Couldn't wake skinny Gemmy again~~

(Editor, January 2017)

You find it hard to come to grips
with what it means to *be a mother*

Keep a straight face
with an eye to writing a poem

You don't *do busy bees*
but on Mondays work in the *School Food Unit Service*
                            (also known as *tuckshop*)

The kids mimic your accent, mime your hand gestures
Your boy pretends he doesn't know you

At home you'll debate whether you qualify as a wog or not

        You are a *peanut*
        The boy refuses to kiss you good night
        The man tells you to stop this nonsense
        You are uptight

Now deal with the *School's Communications Expert*

You find it hard to come to grips
with what it means to *be a wife*

Keep a straight face
with an eye to writing a poem

Night windows
are smudged with inky clouds
of a storm that will not pass

You take the tram in Lygon Street
sweep past the playground
heat-laden footpaths
get off in Spring Street
head to the cool of the Kino

You buy a ticket to *Portrait of a Lady*

At the café order one of those *Little Creatures*

On Saturdays we gather in the grandstand
so like Sunday church

We watch puny players
stream onto the ground
like war heroes
except they fight for teams of metaphors
roos, dogs, hawks, cats, maggies, tigers

At half time, you rage and curse

tiger teasy, mum, it's only a game

At night, your hands nurse
the rainbowing flesh of bumps, bruises, corkers

On Sundays you stay home

Pray for the preservation of brains

The sun swells into a white globe
above the glassy surface of the sea

A dry breeze crawls on the sand, drifting east

Bones, dreadlocks the colour of sea spray
    guides you through new and parallel
                               vocabularies
he knows intimately
(scars and missing teeth account for it)

cushion, custom, deck, flat, handboard, hip, hull, pintail, pod, popout, rail, rocker, twin fin, bowl, break, close out, curl, dead spot, the falls, inside break, lip, peak, pipeline, pump, rip, tube, coffin, ding, drop out, dud, gremmie, hang five, hodad, nose ride, kamikaze, skeg, spinner, soup, wipeout

Goofy foot is your new identity

A kite scans you from the sky
as you sluice into the waves

First time you stand on a board

The boy turns a blind eye
        hangs in salt glare

Deep dark of charcoal on black

Crows circle the sky

Dust plain

Hard-edged dusty walls

Barbed wire

Wing beat of winter

No shadow   Not a tree   No sun   No shade

Inside women do time

> You don't know this yet
> but in two years' time
> you'll teach inside
> where hell
> will pluck you off guard

We abide by two silences
and write from them both

In ash and water
the gateway to dreams
calls to its heart
the gold of a thousand suns
spreading through the leaves
of flowering gums

In their limbs
spirits dwell
sorrows sings

Through lichen and gypsum
moss, clay, crystal
brackens, orchids

The power has gone off: one of these spectacular late summer electric storms. I watch them rolling in from the bay towards us in dramatic Goya swirls of charcoal as though swept by giant brooms. Wait for the spear of lightning that will split the sky in two. The roar of thunder that will make me jump out of my skin and rock the house like a boat tugging at its moorings. I run around. Shut all windows. The man is oblivious to all this. Attacks me with pleasure in his dreams. Rrrr. Rrrr. Rrrr. If it were not for language's impotence, I'd say this is a sweet chainsaw massacre. Light a candle. Pour a glass of Pinot. Enjoy the movement of the hand across the page.

La parole est cette roue de moulin par où sans cesse le désir humain se médiatise en rentrant dans le système du langage.

Speech is that wheel of the mill whereby human desire is relentlessly mediated through entering the system of language.

I work through the night in long hand, shrinking back from the abstract negativity called exile.

Between I and am
is a fish out of water
thin king of oceanic distances

It walks streets unfurling
shadows that augur a poem

Skin encoded with holes
heart ciphered with motives
and metaphors meant merely
to warn the line as it moves
stroke after stroke
promising the resurrection
of the non-ego
as if the sun could take
the hook from my mouth

Along the black smokers of abyssal waters
dig a hole in the ground
open your research satchel
grind a handful of suicide seeds
whip up a bunch of laboratory feathers
sprinkle with dark matter
stir up the wind for more
as do glaze-eyed geneticists
and armchair visionaries

This will obliterate the seasons
and enhance the cycles of the financial year

Discard your conscience

Unless you are an extremophile
set aside a single seed
destined to self-destruct

Welcome to the *twilight of the Anthropocene*

traversals

Tongue a pebble, rock porous as skin, sand
cold hot frost

I feel for words—
grope for the word no

become an aetiological myth

climb the mountain of language
my stone in my mouth

Tongue echo maker
I repeat the words of others

Taciti, soli, sanza compagnia
n'andavam l'un dinanzi e l'altro dopo
come i frati minor vanno per via

In silence and in solitude we went
one first, the other following his steps
as minor friars journeying on the road

I feel words too
much—am the word no

negate all
aetiological myths, teleological truths

Yes, I climb up
the mountain of language, rolling

my stone in my mouth, rolling
me up—listen

Tongue a pebble, rock porous as skin, sand
cold hot frost

*Immagine e ideogramma del mondo
cui ci troviamo a far fronte è lo smog*

An image and ideogram of the world
we face is the fog

Dan zullen de stenen spreken

Then the stones will speak

Flames of memory dig out funnels
in the gardens where we would play and dream

forgetting the slow implosions of progress
the dying trees, the raucous cries of thirsty birds

Wenn du siehst dass der Himmel grün wird
so ist es Zeit für dich aufzustehen, leise

wie Kinder aufstehen
wenn am Morgen Licht schimmert

When you see the sky turn green
so it's time for you to raise, quietly

as children get up
when light shimmers in the morning

And when you think history
is about to crash

in this gorge of grey, green, glib
where once was a whitewashed house—

Quieren que hable...

They want me to speak

Listen

*Cette histoire, filet de mots
asséchés à l'intérieur du sablier*

This story, trickle of dried up
words inside the hourglass

*histoire enflée de celles qui l'ont devancées—
éclats du temps*

story swollen with of those that came before—
shards of time

Tongue a pebble, rock porous as skin, sand
cold hot frost

when hope trickles down to a prayer
in one tongue

Mine is a story of a brilliant defeat
when hope trickles down to a prayer

decrying our impotence
in the face of a drought
spilling out on the land
in the soul and heart

It is a difficult story and it does not end

You will wish you had no eyes to see
no ears to hear. You will wish
you had never been born

I am nothing but trouble
troubling you
nothing but trouble

Listen

I speak of little but inanities on life and death—
the starving of the flesh
wrenching of bones
backstage of the future

I speak of the thin hazy net
over the world like a curse

The heat bows our heads
       bows our heads

   so much I feel

   like a motherless child
       a mother less child

   all babel in limbo

The stars can tell
you everything
                could tell
everything fills
with feverish matter—

my story
is like a book
no one can bear

to read
to the end

for the imploding stars
        exploding suns
             forests of cilia

for the probing of this real myth birthing
a childhood our children's children
will not have

With my stone in my mouth
I climbed up the mountain—crossed
               out
                        Time

Tele-exiled
to a land of little hope

I babble, burble, prattle
                        write the leaving

of creatures, cultures, love, wor(l)ds

this shard of world
we name

Today

The future's backstage

expands and espouses

infinite
                        dreams

that surge and urge

millennia of unnameable

neglect to be

smashed today

Music, murmur of waves crash
nowhere

Music, murmur of waves face
nowhere

Indifferent skies shine in the dark

I speak of the skin of the world
shrivelling inside time's hourglass

it sticks to my skin, feel
how it sticks to yours
this turbulent heat

My story is yours, too

Blind

is how I tell

how your memory will remember
words
like green-house

how your flesh and bones,
more selective, will hold

                                        at bay memory

The body, mere lighthouse

on a rock-hard sea

Identical to this sea, the far one
smoother underfoot

sticks to your skin already

undulating like a plain, hazy, mirage-bound

It is in relief

with sand dunes behind sand dunes
mountains behind mountains

a mountain of cilia
over the voice's well

the idea of metamorphosis that might be
too late

I bend over the well
        feel for the shape of stone

You think that life is ahead

but you don't believe it

You know
our children's worth is

not measured
in elegant formulas
even less so statistics

that bring no bread
even less wine
on the table

It only takes an insect to alert you to your own peril

A prayer of crickets breathing

their silence
in music
against us

Sky turns
from black ink
to blue scribble and scraps flow
into the mouth of the world
until the sun's net

falls

Sea black
like the undersides of my eyelids

We are kept from diving in

Earth, sea of sand

A new sun
shines in the dust

Rivers run
back to their sources

      spring

from our dislocated hands
hollowed out temples

The ground
that bears us
gives off a sulphurous glow

excavates itself out
from under our feet

water is heavy
for drowning souls

the day water went away
the day the earth turned

Thirsty

This century's song

murmurs underground

Silence

multiplies unmultiplies words

sentences made of flesh and bone

white black and every shade

      in between red

Each word is

a bird fretting from star
cross, tree
to star-crossed greed

That dry-eyed rage
in the face of global greed
when the earth breathes its acrid breath

Who wouldn't wish
to blind the world
with a cupful of words
as I do only to drain

fear

reach a place
                    open

to children, love, or say
something much larger

than the heart
exiled in the chest of time

Flux

Silences

flots et sons

sounds and streams

language

se déverse et afflue

flows and pours out

là où le coeur a soif

where the heart is dry

You think that life is ahead
but you don't believe it

Tongue a pebble, rock porous as skin, sand
cold hot frost

when hope trickles down to a prayer
in one tongue

To write a poem
means
nothing

but believing

you have nothing to lose

faultlines

It only takes an insect to alert you to your own peril

A prayer of crickets breathing

their silence
in music
against us

Sky turns
from black ink

to blue scribble and scraps flow

into the mouth of the world
until the sun's net

falls

No sound fits this spectacle   No sound
but the hiss of fire   bark   grass
searing your world into sheer whorls
of alliterations   Hallucinations
of words resounding with nothing

Following faultlines   a gorge aflame
furrows erased in granite and sandstone
          lines of scribble gums forever
receding   The gorge
                    barring you

Now how could I speak again
when syllables shatter on my page
turning words inside out
when letters hover in the air
like the smell of your burning skin?

We were discussing poetics
on our mobiles   How we didn't need
manuals for wordsmiths
preferred to work words as an end
in itself   make a poem fulfilled

in its enaction   look inwards
to the materiality of language
on the page and in the mouth
stress the event   not the effect

You said goodbye

And now I dream that you flit
out of my skin   your voice
lettering me   Poetic enjoyment
perhaps   as if to resist
the etiolation of language

Don't put individual utterances on show
you say   Perform their moves
of repetition   re-use   reiteration
    show your reader the absurd
desire to contain

(...)

For here is the gum and its inferno remains
the grave among blistered roots
the mouthless earth lulling one to leave

If it could speak   it would say
here is the silence   here is the question

This is rock hard country
ridge lip drop cartography

Range on range disarrange
stones steps breath pulse silence

The dark raids blood chambers
you are earth's body

Pulled to the clouds that crush
the idea of sunshine

Corpse hankering after heights
you will forever daydream

Drift in cloud country
settle on crests with souls

Call all the nearly dead
crawling into crevices

This is hard rock country
fringe lip drop cartography

Range on range deranged
stoned steps breath pulse silence

The arkhē appears in the nude

You are ~~I am~~ a tracker bent ~~crouched~~ close to the page ~~ground~~ looking
for traces and signs that sense ~~you~~ has ~~have~~ passed this way

You sniff ~~sniffing~~ for the scent of absence ~~you~~
but above all feel~~ing~~
for the gap in your ~~my~~ life
~~that wants to fill this page~~
~~alone~~

The air is incandescent

The white page ~~track~~ glows

Emptiness talks back talks back talks back
to the heat that cracks open the world ~~ground~~

This is a land of surfeit and lack
of harshness and clarity of image
of absence that opens out
or closes up the world
and sometimes the heart

Smell the rain on the breeze
down at the river mouth
where fishermen stand
in the swirl of incoming waters

Feel the first drops on your skin
where the mystery of the ocean
draws away from salt spray
and the chill of the west wind

Ribbons of kelp sway in the deep

Refracted light dapples your face
        as the child comes up for air

Your hands, useless
                        against the sky

Arms, broken wings
                        skeleton dust

Osprey kestrel tern skua shearwater sandpiper swift

Yellow major swells and heaves
beneath abstracted skies where
angels float across the horizon
casting shadows in the foreground
between you and the sea afire

Textures ebb and flow, ebb and flow
exposing scoured and scarred surfaces
as if time had scraped the body
of the world clean, leaving
filaments of salt in the cracks

You can feel the white hot thing
moulding itself into shape, thrusting
its arms and legs into the corners
of the dissolving canvas, glazing
your eyes and the sand in your heart

When the wide world was still
to be defined by a closed mouth
you'd gather to yourself
hours scattered
in the sun's dry heat
wishing to prise the lips
of a single line open
          prise the flow of time apart

How deeply wrong were your movements
like a sleepwalker's sleeping awake
sleepwalking a wake — sleepworlding
the curved mirror of the page
touching up the backbone of stars

Poems grow in the dark, trace
the descent of sound
into silence

This is a song of silence

This is the sound of the bone
breaking through the skin
of a slow wasting

This is the sound of your breath
lasting through
memory like a mantra

Indigo moon shade
white gardenias
sun bleached hair
the midnight swell
surf sheer gossamer
mood violet
singing mother of pearl

No, it isn't just the wind
whistling in your ears

It is that faraway inside
your head—a whole world
drumming in time drumming
on some utter membrane
holding you

Holding yourself aloft
wings beating about nothing

Tongue echo maker

You sound out the words of others

Taciti, soli, sanza compagnia
n'andavam l'un dinanzi e l'altro dopo
come i frati minor vanno per via

Tongue echo maker

sound a kind of meaning, then force takes over

Art is a medium for the anachronistic
force of the present tense

traces...

We were discussing ecosystems—how they need
time and space, and perhaps a name to exist

You'd pulled out the flyer from the glove box
with your bandaged hand. I imagined it

hurt, the phantom limb. Instinctively pressed
my ticket of leave, as you'd called it

to my breast (a scholarship in human
ecology) knowing we ought to have cleared

the air upon disembarking at Davenport
We pushed on. Filled the car with white noise

Now that ropes of rain drop from another sky
we are trapped between grey walls rising

from the button grass plain, like whales bursting
out from the sea in unbroken succession

to a horizon of waves in a gale. *Traces
are geological,* I say. S*cars man-made.*

You snort. The rain stops. The car coughs on
through absences and shadows, lifting

the weight of silence. The distance grows
between us with each lake, rock-rimmed tarn, river

each valley, hillock, mountain, high plateau
and rusty Queenstown where pyritic smelters

long belched fire and smoke, stripping leaves
off each flaming tree on each flaming hill

The sun, a deep-red gash: Strahan. Night
A near whiteout. Sarah Island, where birds

don't sing for the memories of crushed
skulls, the muted cries of ghosts lashing

past collars and pink ears towards Hell's Gates
And finally, beyond the rugged ranges:

Lake Pedder, barren *nihil* where icy winds pick up
from dry tributaries, erasing dreamtime

They wash towards you as does history
vine-like, tough as scrub, its thorns

carving signs on surfaces, and deeply
beneath roots where god lies tangled

20 September 2015

Acknowledgements

Heartfelt thanks to the editors of journals and anthologies who first published some of these poems sometimes in slightly different form:

Axon: Archive fever
La traductière: Cooking up a storm
                Necromancer
                Fire relies on the leaves of gum trees
Melbourne Writers Festval 2008: Thirst
Not Very Quiet: The expat reconsiders
Poethead: Catch
Recours au poème: Paul Klee on the beach
                Hushed
                Canted bone poem
TEXT: A mourner's riposte
                Traces

My gratitude to Recent Work Press editor-in-chief Shane Strange for his insight and care. Thanks to Recent Work Press too. And thanks to Shane Strange for the cover design.

    Special thanks to Barbara Mobbs for granting me permission to quote from Patrick White's *Voss* as epigraph.

    My thanks also to Bruce Pascoe and Ania Walwicz for permission to cite from their work.

    Individual poems have been reproduced, sometimes in translation, in magazines, on websites and in anthologies, or have been performed at international literary festivals.

    Thanks to the editors of the following anthologies:

Australian Best Poems 2016: Archive Fever
The World Poets Quarterly 2018: Hush
                            Fire relies on the leaves of gum trees
Aesthetica Anthology 2020: Fire relies on the leaves of gum trees

I am grateful to the directors of the literary festivals at which I read individual pieces from this collection in English, French and Spanish and extend my thanks to the translators for their work:

Festival Franco-anglais de poésie, Paris (2008-2019)
Festival International de poésie, Trois Rivières, Quebec (2015)
Festival Internacional de Poesía de Granada, Nicaragua (2019)

'Fire relies on the leaves of gum trees' came third in the Judith Wright Poetry Prize, was shortlisted in the Aesthetica Prize for Creative Writing and earned its author an award for International Best Poets Prize administered by the International Poetry Translation and Research Centre in conjunction with the International Academy of Arts and Letters.

References

There are too many allusions to track in this work. To do so would defeat the peripatetic thrust of the speaker's quest. I have therefore chosen to add a list of references instead of notes. For the same reason, titles of individual poems have been removed from the collection.

The following works inform the journey enacted throughout obliquely or directly. Quotations appear in italics and can be traced as per page numbers:

Blainey, G 1975 *Triumph of the Nomads*. Melbourne: Sun Books.

Blainey, G 1983 *The Tyranny of Distance*. Melbourne: Sun Books.

Blainey, G 1988 *A Land Half-Won*. Melbourne: Sun Books.

Clarke, M 1976 in *Marcus Clarke*, M Wilding ed. St Lucia: University of Queensland Press, p. 645.

Conrad, J 1995 *Heart of Darkness*. Harmondsworth: Penguin, p. 22; 89.

Dante, A 2007 *Inferno*. New York: Anchor. Trans Robert Hollander & Jean Hollander, XXIII, 1-3.

Derrida, J 1998 *Archive Fever: A Freudian Impression*. Chicago: University of Chicago Press. Trans Eric Prenowitz, p. 92.

Drewe, R 1986 *The Savage Crows*. Melbourne: Flamingo.

Franklin, M 1980 *My Brilliant Career*. Melbourne: Angus & Robertson.

Grene, D & Lattimore, R (eds) 1959 *The Complete Greek Tragedies*, vol 2, *Sophocles*. Chicago: University of Chicago Press, p. 59.

Havelock, E 1976 *Origins of Western Literacy*. Toronto: Ontario Institute for Studies in Education.

Kauffman, S 2009 in R E Ulanowicz *A Third Window: Natural life beyond Newton and Darwin*. New York: Templeton Foundation Press, xii.

Kostelanetz, R 2002 *The Gertrude Stein Reader*. New York: Cooper Square Press, p. 108.

Lansbury, C 1970 *Arcady in Australia*. Melbourne: Melbourne University Press.

Malouf, D 1994 *Remembering Babylon*. London: Vintage, p. 9.

Mellamphy, D 2014 'The Twilight of the Anthropocene' http://www.academia.edu/11910814/The_Twilight_of_the_Anthropocene_Welcome_to_the_Electrocene Accessed 21.02.2017

Richardson, H H 1985 *The Fortunes of Richard Mahony*. Harmondsworth: Penguin.

Neilsen, P 1990 *Imagined Lives: A Study of David Malouf.* St Lucia: University of Queensland Press, p. 1.

Pascoe, B 2016 *Dark Emu Black Seeds: Agriculture or Accident?* Boome: Magabala Books, p. 77.

Phillips, A A 1980 *The Australian Tradition: Studies in a colonial culture.* Melbourne: Cheshire-Lansdowne.

Rilke, R M 1983 *Das Stunden-Buch* . Frankfurt: Verlag Herder, p. 94.

Serle, G 1987 *From Deserts the Prophets Come: The creative spirit in Australia.* Melbourne: Heinemann.

Stow, R 1975 *A Haunted Land.* Harmondsworth: Penguin.

Stow, R 1975 *To the Islands.* Harmondsworth: Penguin.

Walwicz, A n.d. 'Wogs', *Mattoid* :13, 16-17.

White, P 1981 *Voss.* Harmondsworth: Penguin.

White, P 1981 *A Fringe of Leaves.* Harmondsworth: Penguin, p. 128.

White, P 1982 *Flaws in the Glass.* London: Jonathan Cape.

Wright, J 1982 *Cry for the Dead.* Melbourne: Oxford University Press.

About the Author

Dominique Hecq grew up in the French-speaking part of Belgium. She now lives in Melbourne. With a BA in Germanic Philology, an MA in literary translation, and a PhD in English, Hecq writes across genres and disciplines—and sometimes across tongues. Her creative works include a novel, three collections of stories, and ten volumes of poetry. Among other honours such as the Melbourne Fringe Festival Award for Outstanding Writing and Spoken Word Performance, the Woorilla Prize for Fiction, the Martha Richardson Medal for Poetry, the New England Poetry Prize, and the inaugural AALITRA Prize for Literary Translation (Spanish to English), Dominique Hecq is a recipient of the 2018 International Best Poets Prize administered by the International Poetry Translation and Research Centre in conjunction with the International Academy of Arts and Letters.

www.ingramcontent.com/pod-product-compliance
Lightning Source LLC
Chambersburg PA
CBHW020326010526
44107CB00054B/2001